MOON SHOT!

For Capri.

Shoot for the moon.
Even if you miss, you'll land among the stars.

- Les Brown

MAPLE ROOTS DESIGN

Neil, Buzz, and Michael are astronauts.

Today these three friends
are flying to the moon!

Before the big day,
to strengthen their legs

Breakfast is served,
steak, toast, and eggs

Mission Control checks for delays

All the controllers give their OKs

"Launch is a go!"
Buckled in tight

the astronauts wait
for their ship to take flight

Let's countdown together!

9 8 7

6 5 4

3 2

BLAST OFF!

The roar of the engines
travels for miles

The astronauts faces
are covered with smiles

Climbing and climbing
with effortless
grace

UP UP UP UP
up into space!

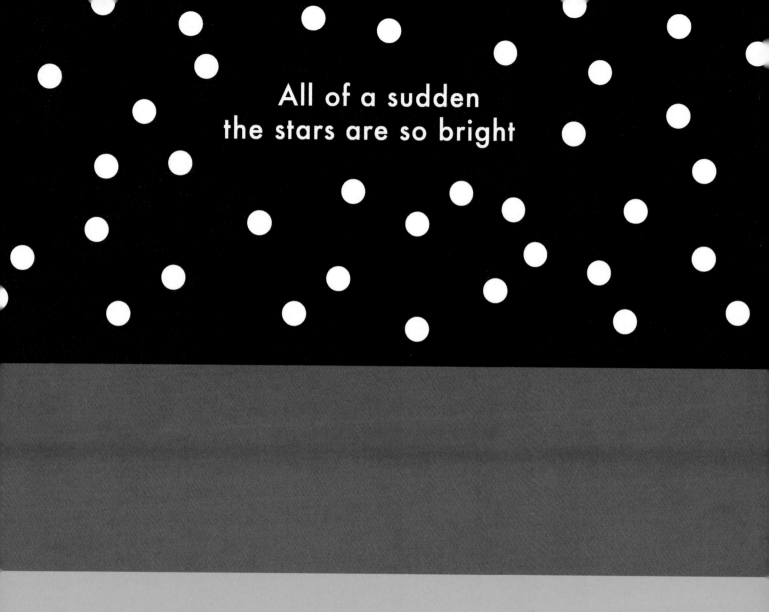

All of a sudden
the stars are so bright

The blue sky of day
has turned into night

The journey would take almost 6 months to drive

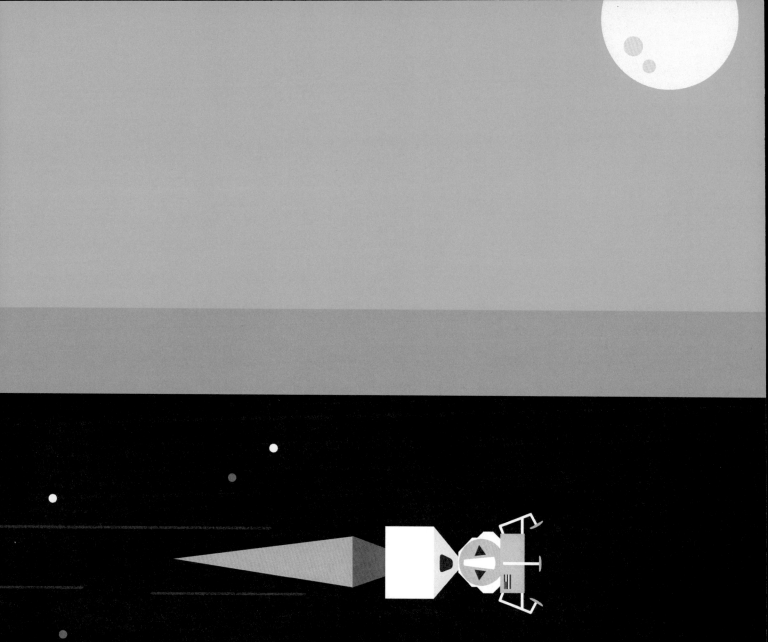

The moon
now so big,
back home
looks so small

They quickly
grab cameras
to capture it all

Michael will stay
and circle around

While Neil and Buzz
fly down to the ground

"All cleared for landing!"
They find just the spot

Kicking up dust,
the jet blasting hot

"The Eagle has landed!"
Neil says to the crew

Right then and there,
their dreams had come true

They climb down the ladder,
leave their spacecraft behind

A small step for man,
a giant leap for mankind

Collecting some rocks,
a salute to the flag

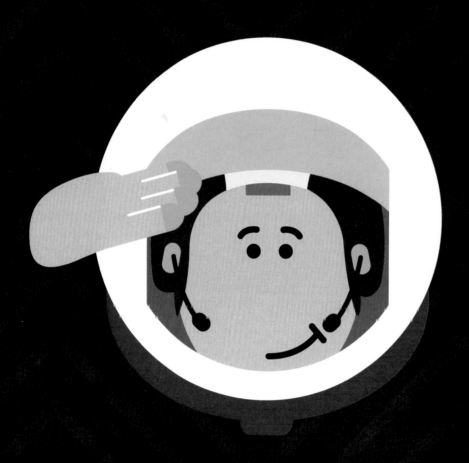

It's time to head back
with their job in the bag

Michael waves,
and greets his two friends

They head back to earth,
as their big mission ends

They speed
through the sky,
say good bye to
the moon

The three
of them know
they'll be home
again soon

A parachute helps to slow down their fall

"Crew signing off!

Thank you to all."

MOON SHOT!

Made in the USA
San Bernardino, CA
26 June 2018